Sir Edmund
Hillary

Sir Edmund Hillary

To Everest and Beyond

Whitney Stewart

With photographs by
Anne B. Keiser

LERNER PUBLICATIONS COMPANY/MINNEAPOLIS

To the Sherpa Children of the Khumbu

Library of Congress Cataloging-in-Publication Data

Stewart, Whitney, 1959–
    Sir Edmund Hillary : to Everest and beyond / Whitney Stewart.
      p. cm.
    Includes bibliographical references and index.
    Summary: Profiles the life of the explorer who, with Tenzing Norgay,
was the first to reach the summit of Mount Everest in 1953.
    ISBN 0–8225–4927–1 (alk. paper)
    1. Hillary, Edmund, Sir—Juvenile literature. 2. Mountaineers—
New Zealand—Biography—Juvenile literature. [1. Hillary, Edmund, Sir.
2. Mountaineers.] I. Title
GV199.92.H54S84 1996
796.5'22'092—dc20
   [B]   95–23028
Manufactured in the United States of America
1 2 3 4 5 6 – JR – 01 00 99 98 97 96

ACKNOWLEDGMENTS

I would like to thank the people whose assistance was invaluable to this book: Sir Edmund Hillary, who graciously gave up many hours for interviews and allowed me to spend a month trekking with him in the Khumbu; Lady Hillary, whose energy and cheerfulness are inspiring; Anne Keiser, without whom I may never have met Hillary and whose photographs add beauty to this book; Hillary's sister, June Carlile, for a great luncheon interview and invaluable follow-up letters; Ang Rita, for his insights, good humor, and dedication to the Himalayan Trust; the late Mingma Tsering, Ang Douli, and their three sons (Ang Rita, Da Tseri, and Temba) for recounting their memories about the Hillary family and for the hospitality in their home in Khunde; Ang Babu for guiding me into the Khumbu; Zeke O'Connor, who entertained me during our race to catch up with Hillary on the Khumbu trails and who was a wealth of information; Mr. and Mrs. Larry Witherbee, who provided dinner and a cozy living room for my first interviews with Hillary; George Lowe, who demonstrated ice stepping in his living room; Rachel Duncan, who helped me find old photos at the Royal Geographical Society in London; Robert Palmer and Leo Dickinson, who let me listen to the tapes of their interview with Hillary; Robert Williams, for his encouragement and hospitality in London; Carl Ryavek, for his geographic knowledge; Naomi Baron and Vickie Lewelling, for their constant support; Christiane Andersson, Lütte Andersson, Yuli Westenberg, Miyuki Yamada, and Megan Clymer, for taking good care of my son while I revised the book; Deborah Short, Neta Robinson, and my careful editors for their comments; and the 1991 fourth grade students at Stoddert School (Washington, D.C.) for their enthusiasm and wise questions.

These people also provided insights about Hillary: Sir Vivian Fuchs, Elizabeth Hawley, Sir John Hunt, Kami Temba, Jan Morris, Lhakpa Norbu, Mingma Norbu, the Thami Rinpoche, Khunde doctors Catherine and Ian, and the Khumjung School staff and students. One last word: I thank my husband, Hans Andersson, for his emotional and editorial support and for enduring my long absences.

—WS

CONTENTS

Tenzing Norgay and Edmund Hillary—the first people to successfully climb Mount Everest

ON TOP OF
THE WORLD

EDMUND HILLARY AND TENZING NORGAY REMOVED
their oxygen masks in silence and gazed at the scene below. From the summit of Mount Everest, the highest peak
in the world, the surrounding peaks of Nepal, India, and
Tibet looked like dwarfs. Edmund and Tenzing were the
first humans to see the world from this point of view.

The two men looked at each other and shook hands.
Then Tenzing opened his arms and embraced the tall,
lanky man whose dreams of ascending Everest had
matched his own. Edmund photographed his partner in
reindeer boots and parka, as Tenzing victoriously held up
an ice ax adorned with the flags of Britain, India, the
United Nations, and Nepal. Tenzing planted the ax into
the icy summit.

Realizing they must save their strength for the descent,
Edmund quickly photographed the landscape on all sides
of Everest. Tenzing, a Buddhist, buried offerings in the

snow—a pencil, some candy—small gifts to the enlightened spirit believed to inhabit *Chomolungma,* Mount
Everest. Edmund remembered to leave a crucifix on be-
half of John Hunt, the leader of the expedition.

After about 15 minutes, the pair began to fumble from
oxygen deprivation. Replacing their oxygen masks, the
climbers quickly retraced their steps downward. They
worried about the small amount of oxygen remaining in
their tanks and the questionable firmness of the ice beneath their boots.

Hillary and Norgay had set out on their final assault
five hours earlier—the morning of May 29, 1953—after
days of chopping steps into solid ice and climbing ridge
after ridge. Hillary later described his thoughts on reaching the summit:

> My first sensation was one of relief—relief that the
> long grind was over; that the summit had been
> reached before our oxygen supplies had dropped to a
> critical level; and relief that in the end the mountain
> had been kind to us in having a pleasantly rounded
> cone for its summit instead of a fearsome and unap-
> proachable cornice. But mixed with the relief was a
> vague sense of astonishment that I should have been
> the lucky one to attain the ambition of so many brave
> and determined climbers....I felt a quiet glow of satis-
> faction spread through my body.

The British expedition team watched the slopes from different camps below. When Edmund's good friend George

Lowe caught sight of the two figures thumping down the trail, he raced to greet them with mugs of hot soup.

"Well," Edmund exclaimed privately to George. "We knocked the bastard off!"

"Thought you must have," said Lowe with a huge grin. The news was quickly released around the world: Edmund Hillary and Tenzing Norgay had become the first people ever to reach the top of Mount Everest.

Worn out from his successful climb, Hillary rests at Camp IV, about 7,800 feet below the summit.

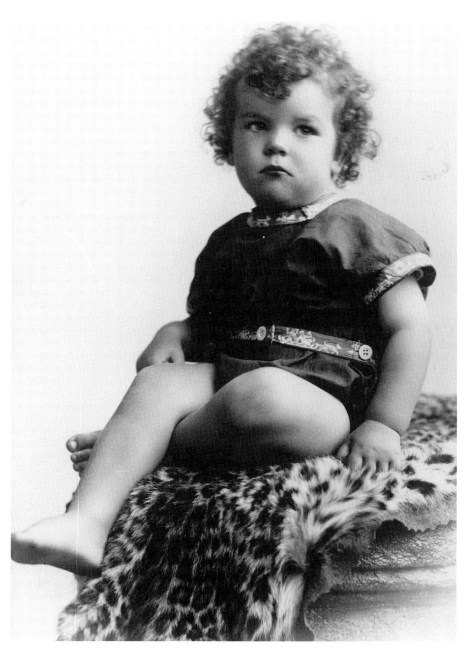

Edmund Hillary, 20 months old

∎

PIONEERING SPIRIT

*Each of us has to discover his own
path. Some paths will be spectacular,
others peaceful and quiet.*

—Sir Edmund Hillary

ON JULY 20, 1919, EDMUND HILLARY WAS BORN
into a New Zealand family that valued the spirit of pio-
neering. On both sides of his family were individuals who
had faced challenge and adventure with determination.

New Zealand was a wild and rugged land, the last sub-
stantial land mass to become inhabited by human beings.
Approximately 1,200 years ago, Polynesian voyagers
landed their wooden canoes on New Zealand's north and
south islands and named their new land *Aotearoa,* Land
of the Long White Cloud. These people, the Maori,
thrived on the islands until Europeans arrived in the

1700s and took over. Middle-class English, in search of new land and resources, set out to colonize New Zealand's 6,200 miles of shoreline. Colonial families, among them Edmund Hillary's ancestors, established pastoral farms to export meat and dairy products to England.

Edmund's relatives on his mother's side of the family were hardworking farmers. His grandparents had a farm in North Auckland and lived off the food it produced. Each child in the family learned to be self-sufficient. Edmund's mother, Gertrude Clark, grew up to be a schoolteacher.

Edmund's paternal grandparents gave birth to a son, Percival Augustus Hillary, who was reading dictionaries by age six. Percival's interest in reading and writing led him to his first job as copy boy for a local newspaper. He was quickly promoted to reporter and photographer.

Percival Hillary and Gertrude Clark married and had two children—June and then Edmund. The family moved 40 miles south of Auckland, to the rural town of Tuakau, and had one more son, Rex. In Tuakau, Percival established a weekly newspaper, the *Tuakau District News*, and became its managing editor.

The Hillarys survived on the products of their farm, as their ancestors had before them. Their seven acres provided them with dairy products, vegetables, and fruit.

Carefree days were rare for the Hillarys. In an effort to teach their children the value of vigorous living, Mr. and Mrs. Hillary kept them busy with household chores and school lessons. The children were rarely allowed to bring friends home after school because Mr. Hillary believed

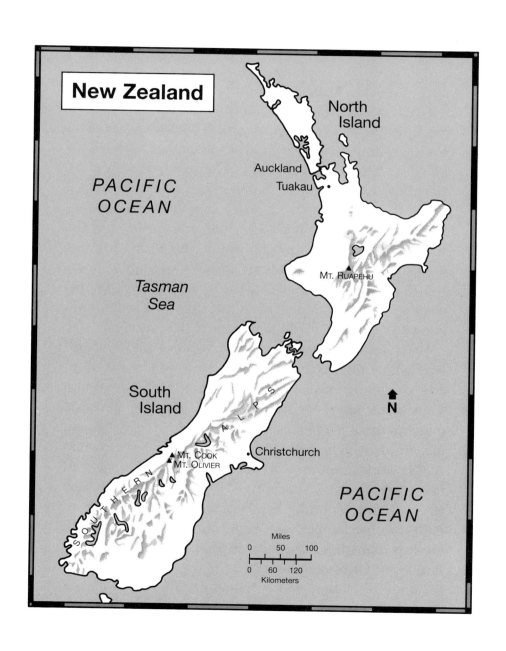

other children would be a bad influence. Edmund, June, and Rex learned to entertain themselves in an "austere but secure existence," as June later described it.

Edmund sought escape from rigid family rules by immersing himself in adventure stories. "Ed was just mad on reading," June said. He would read late into the night, if he could get away with it. June helped her brother by warning him when their father was doing bed checks. Edmund ran a long string down the darkened hallway from June's room to his own. June held one end of the string, and Edmund tied the other end to his big toe. June's room was next to their parents' bedroom, so she was the first to hear their father in the hallway. When he went past her room, June would tug the string so Edmund knew to turn off his light and pretend to be asleep.

When Edmund and Rex played together, they were often competitive. They raced bicycles around their property, drove toy cars, and swung from vines in a swamp. They also fought—with great vigor. Edmund and Rex loved to tease people, especially a pretty young woman named Iris who helped Mrs. Hillary with the housework. As Iris worked, the boys would peek into the kitchen and taunt her. "I see scatterbrain! I see scatterbrain!" they would shout, tempting her to chase them. When Iris finally lost her temper, she would threaten the boys with kitchen utensils or run outside after them. They would race away, far beyond her reach.

Edmund's father had a tremendous ability to work hard. When he wasn't working at his newspaper office, he worked on projects at home. He loved to build things—furniture, a new fence, a tree house, an addition to their home—but his enthusiasm dampened quickly. The Hillarys' home and yard were littered with his abandoned projects.

Mr. Hillary took parenting very seriously and demanded that things be done his way. Once, when he learned that a teacher had punished Edmund at school, Mr. Hillary became furious. He marched down to the school and declared that *he* alone would be in charge of punishing his sons. When Mr. Hillary did decide that punishment was necessary, he took his sons out to the woodshed and spanked them. The children feared their father, until they developed the independence to think for themselves and stand up to him. "My childhood affection for my father became dominated by fear of his discipline and finally by outspoken resentment," Edmund once said.

Edmund never forgot the time his father came roaring into the house, demanding to know who had stolen the best bunch of grapes off a vine that grew in the arbor. When no one volunteered information about the theft, Mr. Hillary took Edmund off to the woodshed. Despite the spanking, Edmund refused to confess. No one ever knew for sure if Edmund had stolen the grapes, but he would not give in to his father, no matter how severe the punishment.

Although Mr. Hillary was strict, he wanted only the best for his children. At meals, Mr. Hillary carefully watched what his children ate. He believed every illness

New Zealand is a rugged country, known for its majestic Alps.

was caused by diet and cured by fasting. If anyone developed a slight cold or flu, he or she was not allowed to eat again until the sickness was past. Mr. Hillary also chose the topics for dinnertime conversation.

Mr. Hillary taught his children to expect nothing free in life and to become self-sufficient as soon as possible. "As a consequence of our upbringing, we all became determined individuals," June said. "Much of Edmund's determination came from standing up to his father."

Later in life, Edmund admitted that perhaps he had deserved some of his father's punishment. "Despite our disagreements, I always had a sense of loyalty to my father and indeed a well-concealed affection. He possessed many qualities that I admired, and even in my most stubborn moments I was never blinded to the fact that I must have been quite a burden on his patience," Edmund wrote in his autobiography. Edmund lived by his father's ideals—that one must be self-reliant and help fellow humans.

Mrs. Hillary shared many of her husband's beliefs, but her demeanor was gentle and openly caring. She kept the family together, listened carefully to the stories and concerns her children shared with her, and instilled in them an awareness of beauty and decorum.

Although the Hillarys worked hard every day, they would settle in for some fun in the evenings. Mr. Hillary often pulled his children next to him in his oversized chair in front of the fireplace and told them fantastic tales about an elflike character named Jimmy Job. He recounted adventures of Jimmy Job's narrow escapes from dangerous tigers and the forces of evil.

Edmund's father also looked after the spiritual development of his children. He became interested in a theory called Radiant Living, preached by a man named Herbert Sutcliff. One of the main principles of Radiant Living was that each person is the master of his or her own fate, the captain of his or her own soul. The family became members of Sutcliff's spiritual society, until Mr. Hillary had a falling out with Sutcliff. Mr. Hillary criticized Sutcliff's plan for communal living, which encouraged young people to quit work, give up their possessions, and live in communal villages. Sutcliff was enraged by the criticism, so Hillary took his family and stormed out, never to return.

> **"I KNEW I HAD MORE PHYSICAL ENERGY THAN MOST AND I REVELED IN DRIVING MYSELF TO THE UTMOST."**

Edmund continued to be interested in philosophy, however, and he read many books about philosophy and religion. He hung onto ideas he admired but never formally joined any religious sect. "I had the feeling I'd been trying to escape from life [with religion]—and that I should go out into the world and get on with ordinary living," Edmund wrote.

School life was another important factor in Edmund's development. At primary school in Tuakau, he was a strong reader, easy to teach. His mother also tutored him at home. Edmund was at the top of his class.

When Edmund was growing up, New Zealand children went to primary school until they were 13 years old. They needed to pass an exam called the proficiency before they were allowed to go on to secondary, or grammar, school. There, they would prepare to attend a university. When Edmund was only 11 years old, his mother insisted that he attend a more demanding school. He passed his proficiency two years before most students even took the exam and then passed the entrance exam for grammar school.

He enrolled in the Auckland Grammar School. Because

the Hillarys were not wealthy, they saved money by having Edmund commute daily by train instead of boarding at the school. He left Tuakau every morning at 7:00 A.M. and returned after 6:15 P.M.

Feeling awkward and insecure on his first day of school, Edmund lined up with 1,200 other students—all older—to listen to the headmaster's opening speech. Then students' names were read aloud, indicating assignment to a particular classroom. Every name was called except Hillary. Not knowing what to do, Edmund asked a teacher, who could not find the name Hillary on any list. Together they went to the main office where they discovered that Edmund had been assigned to one of the lowest level classes. His Tuakau education had not prepared him for the standards of his new school.

The difficult assignments made Edmund fearful. For the first month, he rarely spoke to anyone and often spent his lunch hour alone outside, staring at a busy ant colony. Edmund was no happier in sports than in the classroom. In the first week, the coach took one look at the skinny boy with a protruding rib cage and exclaimed, "What will they send me next!" The coach then sent Edmund to a class for uncoordinated boys—simply because he was thin. The feeling of inadequacy persisted as Edmund grew older. It became one of the reasons he loved to test his strength later in life.

Edmund tried hard but was rarely in good favor with his teachers. In French class, he was punished regularly for poor work and was made to stay after school. This was a sticky problem because Edmund had to catch the evening train. He pleaded his case with the teacher, who told him the only alternative to staying after school was to be spanked with a rod. That's what Edmund chose.

Although Edmund didn't do as well academically as his family had expected, he never got discouraged. He just accepted his situation and relied on himself to get through it. His parents had taught him that life would not always be easy, so he did not expect it to be.

By the time Edmund was 16 years old, however, life had become more bearable. He had grown tall and lean, and he had begun to prove his strength in sports. In 1936 his father agreed to let him go on a class trip to Mount Ruapehu, south of Auckland. This was Edmund's first chance to see snowcapped mountains and feel the rush of wind on his chest. He felt a freedom he had never known before.

After graduating from Auckland Grammar School, Edmund went on to Auckland University, but academic life bored him. He had never outgrown his need for adventure. He bought a motorbike that offered him escape. By this time, Edmund's sister, June, had become an avid hiker, and he began to accompany her and her friends on weekend hikes to the New Zealand foothills.

As he became more enthusiastic about the mountains, Edmund became friends with Jim Rose, a well-known New Zealand mountaineer and president of the New Zealand Alpine Club. Edmund quickly became obsessed with mountaineering, and he and Jim Rose spent hours together discussing the finer points of climbing. Edmund devoured books about mountaineering, many of them written by Eric Shipton, a famous British climber who had ventured to the Himalayas in southern Asia, the highest mountain system in the world. Shipton became Edmund's hero.

Edmund's parents began to worry that their son had no career plans, but his paternal grandmother recognized her grandson's strength. "Don't you worry, Gertie!" Edmund's grandmother told his mother. "He'll surely make something of himself."

The Hillary family in 1938. Left to right: *Rex, Gertrude, Percival, June, and Edmund.*

On top of New Zealand's Mount Sealy, 1947

CONSTANT MOTION

AFTER TWO UNSUCCESSFUL YEARS IN COLLEGE, Edmund dropped out to work on the farm with his father and brother. Mr. Hillary had left his job with the newspaper and turned a beekeeping hobby into a full-time business. He had organized the New Zealand Beekeepers' Association and served as its president. Physical labor was a relief from the suffocation and boredom Edmund had felt in his uninspiring academic life. The fresh air suited him well.

With 1,600 beehives, Mr. Hillary, Edmund, and Rex had more than enough work to do. Every day, seven days a week, the men lifted 90-pound boxes of honeycomb and suffered multiple bee stings. They worked late into the night and took few holidays. Edmund threw himself into the work. "I knew I had more physical energy than most and I reveled in driving myself to the utmost," Edmund wrote in his autobiography.

When New Zealand entered World War II in 1939, Edmund thought about becoming a military pilot. He imagined that flying would be much more exciting than lifting boxes of honeycomb every day. Although his father disapproved, Edmund applied to the Royal New Zealand Air Force. He was accepted, but he had to wait months to start training. During this wait, doubts began to creep into his thoughts. He realized he didn't want to kill anyone—enemy or not. Edmund withdrew his application.

Because the New Zealand government permitted farmers to carry on their work during wartime, Edmund was allowed to continue farming instead of entering the military. This period turned out to be one of the most difficult times in Edmund's life, however. He grew restless and bored with beekeeping and suffered the constant frustration of unfulfilled ambition.

After a period of particularly heavy work, Edmund begged his father for some time off. Because the mountains had always refreshed Edmund, he set out for New Zealand's Southern Alps.

As soon as Edmund reached the Hermitage, a well-known mountain resort, his heart began to race with excitement. Looking up at the frozen ledges and crags, he burned with impatience to climb them. In the lodge that first night, Edmund overheard the conversation of two climbers who had just returned from the 1,000-foot ice cap on top of Mount Cook. Edmund heard only praise for these two men, who were surrounded by adoring young women. He was overcome with disappointment about his own dull life and realized he wouldn't feel fulfilled until he stood on top of a great peak.

The next day, Edmund and a friend named Brian hired a climbing guide to take them up Mount Olivier. To Edmund's dismay, their guide was an aging, overweight man who set a slow pace. The young men learned to kick steps into ice and maneuver an ice ax, but they were impatient to reach their goal. They passed their guide and waited above for him to catch up.

This climb was the first of Edmund's alpine challenges. The sense of satisfaction he felt standing on the mountaintop gave him a taste of personal reward.

By 1942, when Edmund was 23 years old, he had again changed his mind about serving in the military. He reapplied to the air force and was again accepted. He would not learn to be a pilot. Instead, he would become a navigator. The rigorous life in training camp suited Edmund, who was used to hard physical exercise and enjoyed more freedom in the air force than at home. On weekends, he spent hours hiking in nearby foothills, alone or with friends.

Edmund's work as a navigator took him to the Fiji and Solomon Islands in the Pacific Ocean. In his free time, he sailed around uninhabited islands, hiked up rugged mountains, and fished. He was never without adventure. Crocodile hunting became one of Edmund's favorite pastimes. With a friend, Ron Ward, he motored a small boat through muddy lagoons in search of prey. Their greatest catch was an eight-foot crocodile.

Edmund, wearing his air force uniform, with June

When the war ended in 1945, Edmund's air force duties slowed, and military life became mundane. Still seeking adventure, he and his colleagues discovered and repaired an abandoned motorboat, renaming it the *Jolly Roger.*

One morning, Edmund and Ron Ward got up early. They motored the *Jolly Roger* across a bay to drop off a colleague at church. As they were heading back to their base, Edmund sought calm waters so he could drive the boat at full speed. Suddenly, they hit waves, and Edmund heard a loud crack. One of the boat's gas tanks had broken loose, and fire burst through holes around the engine compartment. Both Edmund and Ron were badly burned and prepared to jump ship before the other gas tank exploded. Ron jumped first. Then Edmund let go of the wheel and stood up on the seat. At that very moment, the boat hit another wave and Edmund fell backward on top of the flaming engine compartment. Shirtless, Edmund fried his skin. Finally, he rolled off the boat into the stinging salt water. The *Jolly Roger* blew up in a roar of flames.

The two men were more than 500 yards from shore and nearly delirious with pain. Ron yelled at Edmund to start swimming, but Edmund barely knew where he was. Every few strokes he felt as if he could swim no further and rolled over to float on the waves. Ron had enough strength to encourage Edmund to keep going.

Finally, the two reached shore, where they collapsed on the sand. Doubly scorched by the harsh sun and their burns, they got up and staggered down a road until they met up with two American sailors who took them to a naval hospital. As quickly as possible, doctors gave the wounded men blood transfusions, antibiotics, glucose, and painkillers. By now, Edmund and Ron were delirious.

Three weeks and 140 penicillin shots later, Edmund was released from the hospital with doctor's orders to take life slowly. Taking life slowly was not something Edmund did well.

Not long after Edmund left the hospital, he was discharged from the air force. He was 26. Though he feared losing his independence if he returned to beekeeping, he did return home. He hadn't fully recovered from his injuries but wanted only to go mountain climbing.

For the next five years, Edmund devoted himself to the Southern Alps of New Zealand and gained technical experience that would later prove invaluable. He became friendly with Louise Rose, Jim Rose's teenage daughter, and the two went on mountain outings together.

He also met two men who would change his life. Harry Ayres, a famous New Zealand ice climber, became Edmund's climbing instructor. George Lowe, a schoolteacher, became a lifelong friend and climbing companion. George Lowe remembers their meeting:

> There I was with a six-week holiday job in the mountains, an apprentice under Harry Ayres, when I spotted Hillary on the back seat of a bus. I went up to him and asked who he was. When he told me his name was Hillary, I knew that my father got his queen bees from a man called Hillary up in Auckland. I asked him about it and he said, "Yes, that's my father." I said that I was working under Harry Ayres, and he said that he had just engaged Harry Ayres to take him climbing. So we met on the back seat of a bus.

In 1950 Hillary traveled to Europe with his parents. He visited his sister, June, who was studying in London, and he climbed in the Swiss and Austrian Alps.

Back home in 1951, George Lowe invited Edmund to join a New Zealand climbing team of three men headed for the Himalayas. Edmund used his savings from bee-keeping to pay for the trip. The team flew across the Tasman Sea to Sydney, Australia, then sailed to Ceylon, now called Sri Lanka. From there they took a long, slow train ride up through India. They trekked into the Himalayas and spent weeks along the Tibetan border on high ridges where nobody had climbed before.

This expedition earned Hillary and Lowe a reputation as skilled climbers. They were invited to join a Himalayan reconnaissance trip led by Eric Shipton, Edmund's hero. Edmund jumped at the opportunity. On this trip, the climbers surveyed the southwestern side of Everest, looking for possible routes up the mountain. The reconnaissance trip would prove invaluable to later expeditions—including the one that would make Edmund Hillary famous.

Lowe and Hillary leave Auckland in March 1953 to join the British Everest expedition.

CHAPTER FOUR

GOING BEYOND FEAR

MOUNT EVEREST, OR CHOMOLUNGMA AS TIBETANS and Sherpas call it, stands on the border of Tibet and Nepal. Everest is 29,028 feet at its summit—the highest mountain in the world. The Sherpas, people who moved from Tibet to the Everest area of Nepal more than 500 years ago, have always revered the mountain, believing it to be the abode of an enlightened deity.

Other groups revered Everest too—but not for religious reasons. Many countries wanted to be the first to plant their flag atop Everest. At least 16 men from various nations had died trying. For 30 years, the British had been striving to put a climber on top of Everest. Now they were worried that a team of Swiss climbers would beat them to it.

By 1953 the British Himalayan Committee believed they were close to success. The committee was convinced that the only way to conquer Everest was to send a large, powerful climbing team carrying sophisticated

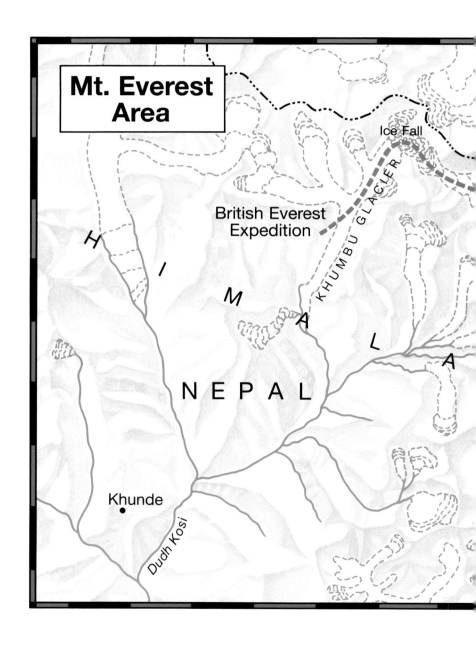

Mt. Everest Area

Ice Fall

British Everest Expedition

KHUMBU GLACIER

H

I

M

A

L

A

N E P A L

Khunde

Dudh Kosi

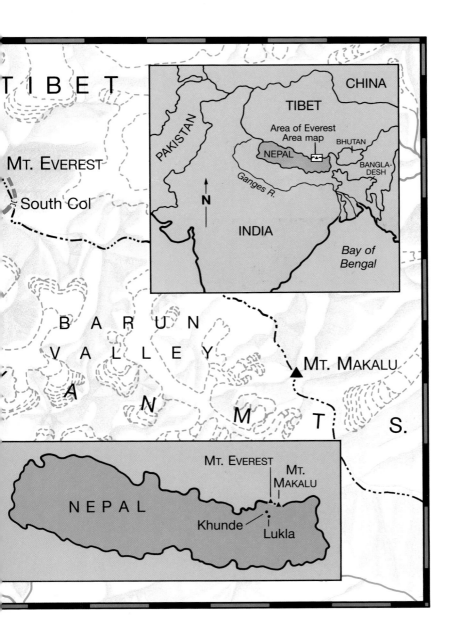

TIBET

MT. EVEREST

South Col

CHINA

TIBET

Area of Everest
Area map

PAKISTAN

NEPAL

BHUTAN

BANGLA-
DESH

Ganges R.

N

INDIA

Bay of
Bengal

BARUN

VALLEY

A
N
M
T
S.

MT. MAKALU

MT. EVEREST

MT.
MAKALU

NEPAL

Khunde

Lukla

gear and modern oxygen systems. Experience had shown that climbers benefited from using oxygen tanks at high altitudes, where the air is very thin. Hundreds of Sherpas would be needed to serve as porters, carrying heavy equipment and assisting the climbers.

The committee first invited Eric Shipton to lead the expedition up Everest. But Shipton did not want to work with hundreds of porters and fancy new equipment. Be-

The British team, front row: *Alf Gregory, George Lowe, John Hunt, Tenzing Norgay, Charles Wylie.* Second row: *Michael Ward, Edmund Hillary, Tom Bourdillon, Mike Westmacott.* Back row: *Thomas Stobart, Griffith Pugh, Wilf Noyce, Charles Evans. One member, George Band, is not shown.*

cause Shipton would not agree to the committee's terms, he was forced out of the leadership role. Captain John Hunt was invited to take over.

The British Himalayan Committee also realized that the climbers would need high-caloric, easily digested food to keep them going in subfreezing temperatures on the mountain. Climbers would have to drink large quantities of fluid as well, or they would quickly become dehydrated in the dry, thin air. The British team purchased special clothing and equipment and high-energy foods such as sardines, canned meat, soup, crackers, oatmeal, raisins, nuts, chocolate, sugar, tea, coffee, and lemonade.

The British press was humming with stories about the expedition. On May 8, 1953, the *Daily Mail* of London commented on the team's chances of success:

> This year's expedition is better equipped than any before. The weather conditions are promising and the newest approach is thought to be not quite so difficult as that which used to be followed.
>
> Some experts rate the chances of success as higher than usual, while others think that they are about even. It would be a mighty achievement if, after 30 years of striving, the British flag could be planted on that demonic summit.
>
> There would be no material gain, no territory won or treasure garnered—nothing except the joy of achievement and the knowledge that man's unconquerable spirit had accepted another challenge and had again conquered.

John Hunt had to put together a team of climbers who were personally motivated. But only two men would actually be sent to the top of Everest—the rest would support them from lower camps on the mountain. Hunt wanted men who would not question his final decisions about the summit assault team.

He purposely mixed the ages of the group members, believing that "young tigers" could add force and energy to the steady, dedicated strength of older members. The most important characteristic of each candidate was temperament. Hunt could not risk choosing a climber whose personal ambition might get in the way of team cooperation. Both Edmund and George Lowe were chosen, having proven their skill and team spirit during the Himalayan reconnaissance trip with Eric Shipton in 1951.

Before setting out from New Zealand for the 1953 expedition, Edmund had to pass a physical exam. When Dr. Stuart Watson of Auckland entered the examination room, Edmund explained that he was on his way to climb Mount Everest and needed a doctor's confirmation of fitness. Dr. Watson was a bit stunned, not at all sure how to judge if a man was fit for Everest.

"You're aiming a bit high, aren't you?" Dr. Watson asked as he began checking Edmund's ears, eyes, nose, and chest. "Have you been climbing much these days?"

Edmund told of his climbing adventures, specifically time spent in the European Alps.

"How did you find the climbing there?" the doctor continued.

Mount Everest—the tallest mountain on earth

"Too easy! Too easy!" exclaimed Edmund. With that, Dr. Watson decided that this enthusiastic man was probably as ready as anyone to climb Everest.

Edmund and George Lowe joined Hunt's team, along with eight British climbers and one Sherpa climbing expert, Tenzing Norgay. Norgay would act as both climber and *sirdar,* leader of local guides and porters. Also with the team were physiologist Dr. Griffith Pugh, photographer Thomas Stobart, and news correspondent James Morris. Helping the expedition was a company of 350 Nepalese porters who would assist in every way: carrying 100-pound loads, setting up and breaking camp, cooking meals, brewing thousands of cups of tea and hot lemonade, and telling jokes to keep spirits high.

> **"WASHED IN SOFT MOON-LIGHT THE SPLENDID MOUNTAINS STOOD...AND GIGANTIC ABOVE ALL, EVEREST ITSELF."**

Today, most Himalayan climbers and trekkers fly up to the Lukla airport, altitude 9,000 feet, and start trekking from there. In 1953, however, the Lukla airport did not exist. Climbers had to walk up the Kathmandu Valley and bear intense tropical heat and humidity before facing frosty winds and snowstorms in the mountains.

By March 1953, the team members had convened in Kathmandu—the capital of Nepal—to ready themselves for the 170-mile trek from the Kathmandu Valley to the Everest region. The men gathered at a hotel and planned their early strategies.

On March 10 at Bhatgaon—10 miles east of Kathmandu, where the road ends—the 1953 Everest team began its trek. They ascended slowly, covering approximately 10 miles per day. They shared the route with Nepalese onlookers and could not even go to the bathroom without an audience. Millions of local children in frayed clothing watched as Hunt's team set up camp in potato fields edged with rhododendron trees.

At the start of the expedition, Edmund was impatient with the slow pace of the team. He would race up the trail, only to find himself bored, waiting for the others who followed with tents and food. Photographer Tom Stobart commented on the personal styles of the climbing group: "Everyone had their own system. Those bitten with the full spirit of one-upmanship would jostle for the lead like contestants in a walking race."

Edmund was certainly bitten. He helped the team in any way he could, but his eye was set on Everest's summit. Both he and Tenzing Norgay were full of competitive energy. But keeping their dreams to themselves, they showed great cooperation.

George Lowe took time out to entertain the team members. Just for a laugh, Lowe would don huge magnolia blossoms on his head or take out his false teeth. Even the energetic Sherpas joined the fun; their favorite prank was to take down the tents while the climbers were still inside them.

Up the trail about 7,000 feet, climbers began to encounter walls of *mani* stones, engraved with the Tibetan Buddhist prayer *Om Mani Padme Hum,* "Hail to the Jewel of the Lotus." The Sherpas worshipped at these walls and always walked around them clockwise—going with the flow of life. The climbers showed respect for the Sherpas by passing the walls clockwise even when the trail was narrow and risky. The team entered small villages of whitewashed mud houses adorned with colorful flags. More Buddhist prayers were printed on the flags.

Walls of mani stones, inscribed with Buddhist prayers, lined the trail as the men climbed.

Everywhere, team members were reminded of the strong spiritual life of the Sherpas.

Large goats called Himalayan tahr scampered over the slopes, yaks bellowed and grunted in their pastures, Impeyan pheasants hid their electric blue feathers behind juniper trees, Sherpa songs floated upward from the potato fields, and the mystical music and foghorn chanting of Buddhist monks poured out of small temples.

Sixteen days after setting off on foot, the party reached Tengpoche Monastery, where 300 porters dumped their loads. John Hunt chose a spot next to the monastery for a rear base camp. There, he would set up radio equipment for contact with higher camps and set up scientific equipment. While trying to scale Everest, the team would also use this opportunity to study oxygen deprivation, high-altitude nutrition, and mountaineering medicine.

Beneath the dazzling mountain peaks, the team was surrounded by richly scented pine and juniper trees. Curious Sherpas came to watch the climbers in their constant activity, planning for the challenge ahead. Everyone celebrated setting up the first base camp by drinking bowl after bowl of *chang,* Tibetan rice beer, to wash down roasted potatoes.

For the next two weeks, team members climbed up and down glaciers and small peaks, conditioning themselves for the steep climbing and thin air to come. Camp life was demanding, and the men had to demonstrate patience with crowded conditions, constant chill, altitude-induced headaches, and bland food that always tasted a bit like burning logs, yak dung, and juniper branches from the open fire. Many things kept the climbers awake: the snoring and coughing of others, tents flapping in the wind, and cold air seeping inside. The men were also troubled by various ailments caused by high altitude: stuffy noses, dizziness, indigestion, frostbite, sore throats, boils, and nausea. The beardless Tom Stobart complained that living conditions were so cramped that beard clippings from other team members had fallen inside his camera equipment.

Leader John Hunt chose Edmund to take a party up the Khumbu Glacier. There, Edmund would establish an upper base camp and then find a route up the glacier's icefall—a jagged ice formation resembling a frozen waterfall. This small advance team—Hillary, George Lowe, George Band, and Mike Westmacott—was assisted by 38 porters. Theirs was no small task—to mark off the route and set up a line

Hillary and a Sherpa porter painstakingly climb an icefall at about 19,000 feet.

of camps where food and shelter would be deposited. On April 12, the party found an uncomfortable but mildly satisfactory location for the upper base. The ground was covered with sharp rocks; icicles hung from trees.

Tom Stobart was unhappy about the new campsite. In his book he recalls the feelings he had when he reached the site: "It is a cheerless place, a loveless place, even an ugly place, and very far from home. But somehow it has to be made into a home."

James Morris, newspaper correspondent for the *London Times,* described the scene differently: "a moon landscape, little touched by the warmth of humanity. At night the scene was breathtakingly beautiful. Washed in soft moonlight the splendid mountains stood, with the mysteries of Tibet ever pulsing beyond them...and gigantic above all, Everest itself."

After the upper base camp was settled, Hillary and his team climbed higher to set up Camp II. Leading the team into the icefall was tricky. The men had to place aluminum ladders over threatening crevasses and cut a path up the craggy ice. Edmund later described the uneasiness of sleeping in Camp II: "It was quite eerie in this camp at night—we were always aware of movement as the icefall shuddered its way downward—and aware too of the unstable ice above us."

For days, Edmund and the other climbers relayed equipment higher and higher, establishing more camps at intermediate locations. Their work was tiring, and the men could never be too careful. Once, when Edmund and

Tenzing were tied to the same climbing rope and racing down the mountain from Camp III to Base Camp, Edmund took a great leap onto an ice block that broke off and took him with it. Only Tenzing's quick rope work saved Edmund from disaster.

"Without Tenzing, I would have been finished today," Edmund told the team members back in camp.

It was the last week of April. At 26,000 feet, the team reached the depression of the South Col, which opened up to Everest's southeast ridge—the last ridge before the summit. Plotting the final stages with exactitude, John Hunt sent teams of men out to test their stamina and oxygen systems.

Norgay and Hillary in camp

The team carried closed and open oxygen systems. Both were bulky units, strapped to the climbers' backs. The closed system allowed climbers to breath only pure oxygen through a mask; the open system allowed them to breath a mixture of pure oxygen and outside air.

Following this final reconnaissance, Hunt called a meeting in a large pyramid-style tent. There he would announce the final assault teams that would try for the top. James Morris later described the excitement:

> It was a memorable occasion even for climbers inclined towards a certain phlegmatism [sluggishness].... Snow fell heavily on the little camp as Hunt announced his plans, and the canvas of the tent flapped monotonously in the wind. Around the packing cases that formed a table sat as tense and as watchful a group of men as ever a tent held.

A successful expedition would depend on team spirit and cooperation. Hunt later reflected on this idea: "I should like to stress the unity of our party. This was undoubtedly the biggest single factor in the final result....It would be difficult to find a more close-knit team than ours....Everyone rightly believed that he had a vital part to play in getting at least two members of the team to the top."

The men were silent as Hunt explained his plan, each man keeping to himself his thrill or disappointment. Hunt's plan was to send two assault teams to the top. Tom Bourdillon and Charles Evans were to move up first, using the closed oxygen system that was still new and untested. This pair was to try and reach the South Summit—1,328 feet below the final summit. If by chance they could go on, they would try for the top. Following behind would be Edmund Hillary and Tenzing Norgay, equipped with the open oxygen system. A support party would carry most of the equipment, allowing the summit pair to save energy. The support party would also set up a final camp as high as possible on the southeast ridge.

On May 26, Bourdillon and Evans, followed by John Hunt and a Sherpa named Da Namgyal, set out from the South Col. Hunt and Da Namgyal climbed to 27,350 feet and left a tent and food there for Edmund and Tenzing. Evans and Bourdillon, handicapped by a broken supply valve on an oxygen system, continued higher in the face of a miserable blizzard. By 1:00 P.M., they had reached the South Summit. They could have gone on to the final summit, but it was too late in the day for a safe return to camp. Slowed by weather and failing equipment, the pair turned back. Quiet as they were about their disappointment, Evans and Bourdillon contributed to the eventual success of the team. They had broken the trail higher than anyone had climbed before; this gave Edmund and Tenzing confidence that the final summit was within reach.

But before Edmund and Tenzing could set off, a dark blizzard blew in. The climbers were tent-bound, frustrated, and bored. Though the high altitude had taken away their appetite, the men forced themselves to sip hot lemonade and nibble crackers and canned sardines. Inside the tent, freezing and drowsy, the men shared novels, wrote journal entries, and daydreamed about the peak above.

Finally, on May 28, the weather cleared. Edmund and Tenzing pushed on again, supported by George Lowe, Alfred Gregory, and Sherpa Ang Nima. While the rest of the team waited below with anxiety, the assault team trudged over the ridge, cutting steps into the ice and often falling into waist-deep snow traps. Their immediate difficulty was in finding a suitable camp.

On and on they went, tiring with every step. Finally, they stopped at an altitude of 27,900 feet and settled onto a small pitch. This site, Camp IX, was at that time the highest camp ever set in the history of climbing. Gregory, Lowe, and Ang Nima did not dally there but turned back, in a hurry to get down before they used up all their oxygen. Edmund later reminisced about his experience at Camp IX: "It was with a certain feeling of loneliness that we watched our cheerful companions slowly descending the ridge, but we had much to do."

Eating and sleeping were nearly impossible for Edmund and Tenzing. They spent two hours trying in vain to level the tent; they had to pitch it on an uneven ice floor. With a temperature of −17° Fahrenheit, the two men stayed awake most of the night, feeling the sharp gusts of wind against their tent.

Between 3:30 and 4:00 the next morning, May 29, the men stirred. Tenzing set about making hot lemonade while Edmund pulled the gear together. To his dismay, the boots he had left outside his sleeping bag all night had frozen solid. He was forced to spend the next two hours thawing them over the camp stove. Edmund was angry about the delay and worried that his feet might freeze.

At 6:30 A.M., the two men set off up the mountain. Tenzing took the lead, giving Edmund the chance to follow slowly in his stiff boots. After a while, Edmund took over the exhausting procedure of cutting steps out of the ice in front. Back and forth, the men took turns at the lead, each man supporting the other with a rope. By 9:00 A.M., they reached the South Summit, where they rested for ten minutes. Each man kept silent with the fear of unstable ice underfoot.

The last 300-foot slope looked dangerous. In fleeting moments, Edmund thought of turning back. Then he reminded himself that this was Everest and that extra effort must be made. He was later heard to say, "It is not the mountain we conquer, it is ourselves. If you can overcome your fear, you are frequently able to extend yourself far beyond what you normally regard as your ability."

After another hour, the men faced a new obstacle: a 40-foot vertical ice crack. Each man had to wedge his backpack and himself up the crack. The physical and mental strain robbed them of energy. Breathless and panting, they rested a moment at the top of the crack. "For a few minutes I lay regaining my breath and for the first time really felt the fierce determination that nothing now could stop our reaching the top," Edmund later recalled.

Surmounting the rock pinnacle, they carried on, ever vigilant of their oxygen levels and stopping at times to

Tenzing Norgay plants a flagpole on the summit.

chip ice off their breathing apparatuses. Hour after hour, the men cut steps into the ice and pulled themselves over ridge after ridge. The lifting and stepping seemed endless.

Following each rise and fall of the trail, they finally arrived at a large hump. Suddenly, they realized there was no more mountain above them.

On May 29, 1953—at 11:30 A.M.—Edmund Hillary and Tenzing Norgay stepped onto the summit of Everest.

The climbers are honored for their achievement by India's prime minister.

MEDIA CRAZE

THE SLOW TREK OFF EVEREST AND DOWN INTO THE Kathmandu Valley gave Edmund, Tenzing, and the entire Everest team a glimpse of the world's excitement over the conquest of Everest. As the men sloshed through mud and thirsty leeches, mail carriers raced up the trail to bring the team packs full of congratulatory letters and telegrams.

A great surprise came when Hillary was handed a letter from John Hunt, who had gone on ahead to make travel arrangements from Kathmandu. The letter was addressed to Sir Edmund Hillary K.B.E.—Knight Commander of the Order of the British Empire. Hillary assumed the title was a joke until he read the letter, only to discover that the Queen of England had knighted him and Hunt for their accomplishments on Everest—Hunt for his leadership and Hillary for the summit attack. (As a New Zealander, Hillary was a citizen of the British Commonwealth.)

Hillary was horrified. He was honored, but he had never liked titles. Now he had one and felt nothing but dismay. Hillary later told an American interviewer that he was not "knightly material."

Meanwhile, Indian and Nepalese reporters had picked up the story of the final assault and were claiming that it was Norgay who had done the work of climbing—Norgay who had stepped on the summit first—and Hillary who had dragged along behind his Sherpa guide. Norgay never made this claim.

The reporters also questioned why Norgay had not been knighted along with Hillary and Hunt. Later reports clarified that the British had not knighted Norgay because he was not a citizen of the British Commonwealth. Norgay had been raised in Nepal but had later moved to Darjeeling, India. Thus, both Nepal and India claimed Norgay as a national, and Great Britain didn't claim him at all.

Reporters all wanted to claim success for their own countries. The climbers, however, explained that team effort had made the expedition successful, and no single climber could claim success for himself or his country alone.

More trouble started with the media because the story of the expedition's success was sent exclusively to the *Times* in London. The British and New Zealand team members had signed a contract allowing the British newspaper to break the story to the world. Many Indian and Nepalese reporters were angry that the story had not been provided to them at the same time as the British. They tried to get statements from Tenzing because he had not signed the contract. Some reporters went so far as to say that Tenzing had been bribed to keep quiet until Britain announced the team's success. Tenzing denied the accusation.

Another reason for the trouble was political. Nepal and India had once been under British colonial rule—but were no longer. Now the people of these countries wanted to show their independence from Great Britain. Tenzing, who was pushed and pulled by journalists and nationalists from east and west, became an unwilling pawn in political games.

Sir John Hunt and Sir Edmund Hillary—Knights of the British Empire

No matter what the climbers did or said, they couldn't slow down the media blitz. When the team reached the road to Kathmandu, they were attacked by well-wishers— most of them wanting to touch Tenzing. Hoards of men, women, and children pushed Tenzing into an open jeep, showered him with flowers, and ran beside him as the jeep tried to maneuver through the crowded street. The rest of the team followed in jeeps or on foot. Celebrations and speeches were made, but not without more angry statements by reporters and ill feelings on the part of team members and locals.

When the team reached Kathmandu, government officials and the king and queen of Nepal took over the honors. After that, the entire team was greeted warmly. When they traveled on to India, they were mobbed again, and the prime minister, Jawaharlal Nehru, arranged a reception.

Everywhere the men went, there were cheers and media attention. They traveled back to England, where Hillary and John Hunt were knighted in a private ceremony attended by team members and the British royal family. For the next two months, team members were guests of honor in many social circles, eating smoked salmon and drinking champagne as never before. Hillary had become very thin on the expedition. Now he ate as if he had an empty leg.

In August Hillary and George Lowe flew back to New Zealand to celebrate with their own families and members of their own country. The only peace they found was on airline flights. En route to Auckland, Hillary made a stop in Australia to visit his old friend Louise Rose, who was now studying at the Sydney Conservatorium of Music. The short time they spent together in Sydney was not relaxing, however. Reporters followed them, wrote about their probable romance, and predicted marriage.

After Hillary went on to New Zealand, journalists continued to follow Louise, demanding to know when she would marry Edmund Hillary. In distress from all the publicity, Louise called her parents in New Zealand and then spoke to Hillary, who happened to be visiting at the Roses' home. Over the telephone, Hillary asked Louise to marry him and to travel to England with him on an upcoming lecture tour. She accepted.

With only nine days to plan the wedding, Louise's life was an excited blur. The couple was married on September 3, Louise's 23rd birthday. George Lowe was Edmund's best man. Edmund and Louise exited the church under an archway of ice axes. When Hillary later wrote in his autobiography about his marriage, he declared happily, "It certainly proved the most sensible action I have ever taken."

The morning after the wedding, Edmund and Louise took off for England, accompanied by George Lowe. On this honeymoon of a different sort, Edmund gave lectures while Louise charmed reporters, hosts, and guests at every stop.

"I am not sure if I'm dreaming everything or not....Life is really too good to be true," wrote "Lady Hillary" in a letter to the Hillary and Rose parents.

When Edmund's sister, June, first met her new sister-in-law, she thought Louise was cheerful and kind—but very innocent. During part of Edmund's travels, Louise stayed in Norfolk, England, where June now lived with her husband, Jimmy Carlile. June and Jimmy both felt they had to protect Louise from hungry journalists. But Louise adjusted quickly to her new life as Lady Hillary.

Through England, Belgium, Denmark, Finland, Iceland, and the United States, the Hillarys drew audiences.

Edmund and Louise at their wedding reception in Auckland

People enjoyed meeting Louise as much as they liked meeting Edmund. He was often shy and was quite happy to let his wife become the protective front—a role she would play for the rest of her life. She stayed calm during photo sessions and socialized enthusiastically, even when Hillary went off in some corner to relax.

The pace of Edmund Hillary's life had been turned up, rarely to wind down again. After the Everest lecture tour, the Hillarys returned to Auckland to begin a comfortable married routine. Six weeks later, however, Hillary could not resist the excitement of heading off again to Nepal, this time to lead a New Zealand Alpine Club exploration of the Barun Valley, east of Everest. Although he loved living with his new wife, Hillary still yearned to climb the many untouched Himalayan peaks.

Hillary prepares for the Antarctic expedition. A support plane sits behind him.

CHAPTER SIX

TRACTORS TO THE POLE

FOLLOWING THE EXPEDITION TO THE EAST OF Everest, Hillary settled at home in Auckland with Louise. Because he did not receive a salary for his mountaineering expeditions, he returned to keeping bees with his brother, Rex. He also wrote a book about his climbing experiences, entitled *High Adventure.* To keep his spirit happy, he took to the Southern Alps of New Zealand. There, he climbed Mount Magellan.

Hillary also had a new kind of pleasure: fatherhood. The Hillarys' first child, Peter, was born in 1954. Domestic life was temporarily satisfying.

The routine was not to last long, however, because Hillary was invited to join a New Zealand team on what the media called "The Last Great Journey in the World"— a trans-Antarctic expedition led by Sir Vivian Fuchs, a British geologist and explorer.

Fuchs's team would depart from England and sail to

*When he left for
Antarctica, Edmund
temporarily said good-
bye to beekeeping with
Rex (right).*

Antarctica. There, the team would make the first over-
land crossing of the continent by tractor—from Shackleton Base on the Weddell Sea, through the South Pole, to
Scott Base on McMurdo Sound. The New Zealand team
would act as support by finding a suitable land route for
Fuchs's tractors from the pole to Scott Base and by establishing supply depots along that route. After Fuchs

A beaming Edmund shows off his new son, Peter.

passed the pole, he would continue his journey, using food and fuel left by the New Zealanders.

At first, Hillary was hesitant to join the trans-Antarctic team because he couldn't envision his role in it. Fuchs appeared to be a serious man whose purpose wasn't just to prove his ability to withstand the hardships of the polar region but also to undertake scientific study in areas

of glaciology, radiation, meteorology, and human physiol-
ogy. "You should never undertake a journey of this nature
to wild places without an objective," Fuchs explained.
"One should never go from A to B just for the record, but
rather because you're trying to find out something."

Hillary was a man of adventure, not science. He could
not see how a skilled mountain climber might assist a scientific expedition. But New Zealand wanted to play a
part in this grand expedition. The New Zealand government contributed $120,000 to the project and decided to
appoint a team to represent the country. They formed the
Ross Sea Committee and formally invited Hillary to become the team leader. After careful consideration and
much discussion with Louise, Hillary agreed to help. His
good friend George Lowe would also be involved in the
expedition.

By 1955 Hillary was deeply involved in planning his
support effort. During this active time, Louise had another baby—this time a girl named Sarah. Hillary felt sad
that he would soon have to leave his growing family.

The expedition would be dangerous. Driving tractors
across Antarctica could be as risky as moving through a
mine field. Bridges of snow could easily disguise large
crevasses. An advance group with a sled-dog team,
lighter and swifter than the tractors, would be needed to
test the depth of the ice and snow and mark the route
with flags. Controlling 80-pound dogs—all tied together,
growling, and pulling at their harnesses—would be no
easy task.

Snow blindness and subzero temperatures were also a threat. The sun never sets during the Antarctic summer. If an explorer were to go outside without goggles, day or night, ultraviolet rays reflected off the snow could damage his eyes in a short time. If a team member were to work outside for a long time without proper clothing, he would risk frostbite or death from exposure.

Danger was just one element to consider before the team set out. Another was equipment. Explorers like to use well-known and trusted equipment for their trips, but at the same time they want to try out new technology that can help advance scientific knowledge. Fuchs planned to include both kinds of equipment.

On November 14, 1955, Fuchs set out from England on a ship called the *Theron.* Small groups of well-wishers cheered and waved from wharves and jetties. This trip would launch an advance team that would stay over the long, dark winter in Antarctica and set up a base camp.

To gain experience in the polar region before leading his own team, Hillary joined the ship when it landed in the Cape Verde Islands (off the coast of Africa) before heading across the equator to Montevideo, Uruguay. For more than a month, the ship headed toward the Antarctic, finally reaching the icy Weddell Sea on December 22.

As the ship moved into a sea of packed ice, progress slowed. Soon the ship halted in deep ice. The sky grew overcast, and reconnaissance became impossible. Using ax, shovel, and boat hook, the crew spent hour after hour, day after day, trying to free the ship. As some men hacked large chunks of ice from in front of the boat, others pushed the ice toward the stern and into the wake behind the propeller.

For 33 days, the ship was stalled. Patience grew thin. The expedition lost precious time, and when it finally reached the Filchner Ice Shelf, where the base was to be built, the crew had to work in round-the-clock shifts to unload tractors, scientific equipment, and rations. They moved nearly 300 tons of equipment to the base site.

While the crew carried supplies, pilots took turns flying reconnaissance flights inland to record topographical information. Later, planes would be used to deposit supplies at depots and to evacuate men during medical emergencies.

The end of the Antarctic summer was upon them (December, January, and February are summer in the Southern Hemisphere), and the *Theron* had to leave quickly before frozen seas imprisoned the ship. A team of only eight men would stay to set up the Shackleton Base during the dark winter months. Amid smiles and laughter, the teams said farewell to each other, but most of the men felt regret. Hillary, like the others who were leaving, felt as if he were abandoning his colleagues. The men who were staying could already feel their isolation. Sir Vivian Fuchs later described the sad parting:

> Theron slid slowly away from the ice edge while three long blasts of the siren drowned the final shouts of farewell, and we found ourselves silently waving to the tiny cluster of men quickly dwindling in size until individual figures could no longer be distinguished.

Nobody could have predicted that while Hillary and Fuchs were back in their homes, planning the crossing, the eight men in the winter party would face terrific blizzards that would wash away all of their coal and much of their food. Due to bad weather, the men were unable to build proper shelter, so they lived in a packing case from a Snow Cat, which was not much bigger than the vehicle itself. There was always an inch of ice on the floor, and condensation from the men's breath and cook stoves formed stalactites, which hung like icicles from the ceiling.

The men fabricated an oven, using an empty oil drum insulated with fiberglass. They also became inventive

An Antarctic team member digs out after a blizzard buries his camp in snow.

with their cooking—anything to avoid drab meals. One innovative cook served peas with a hint of mint; he dropped a dab of toothpaste into the pot of boiling peas.

The men felt the misery of jumping into icy sleeping bags every night and sleeping in −63°F temperatures. Morning after morning, month after month, they had to dig out their accommodations and rescue dogs from snow drifts. During the day, they worked at building a base station.

Back in England, in December 1956, the day before Fuchs set sail again for Antarctica, his crew was graced with a visit from Queen Elizabeth II. She stayed for tea. The next morning, Fuchs and his crew set off in a Danish polar vessel, the *Magga Dan,* from the Tower Bridge in London. They sailed until January 23, 1957, when they rejoined the lonely team on the Filchner Ice Shelf.

For Hillary's New Zealand team, there were still great preparations to be made. Hillary's men would be equipped with five modified farm tractors, but he wanted more vehicles. An American admiral stationed in Antarctica agreed to give the New Zealanders two snow vehicles called Weasels. Hillary also needed six dog teams, for a total of 60 sled dogs. The Auckland Zoo bred some Huskies and imported other dogs from Greenland and the Australian Antarctic base.

Just before Christmas in 1956, shortly after Fuchs had departed with the British team, Sir Edmund Hillary stood on the deck of the *Endeavor* with tears on his cheeks, waving good-bye to his wife and two small children. He would be away from them for more than a year—which made this dangerous expedition to Antarctica even more difficult for him.

Once they reached McMurdo Sound on the Antarctic continent, Hillary's team established Scott Base at Pram Point on Ross Island, not far from the American base at Hut Point. There, they loaded a reconnaissance plane that would fly over and examine the terrain and deliver supplies to interior depots.

On March 5, Hillary made his first radio contact with Fuchs and George Lowe, who were setting up their base camp on the other side of the continent. They compared notes about the challenges the teams were encountering on both sides.

Hillary and his team kept busy throughout the winter (June, July, and August in Antarctica), preparing supplies, making plans, and trying out the tractors. On one trial run, Hillary's tractor broke through the ice and had to be dug out. The team was next delayed by soft snow and bad visibility. Day after day, team members had to spend hours digging out tractors and steering around menacing crevasses.

Riding the tractors was miserable when the temperature hit –30°F because the riders had no protection from the cold and wind. When they became too chilled, the men would jump off their seats and run alongside the tractors to warm themselves. In desperation, Hillary rigged up a "caboose" for riders behind one of the tractors. It was a 12-foot by 4-foot cabin on skis, with bunks, a cupboard, a cookstove, and a radio.

Wherever they were, the men were active. Outside, they fixed tractors and cleared trails. Inside huts and tents, they washed dishes, melted snow for hot drinks, and refueled heaters and stoves. When the men finished their work, they could relax in their "library" or make radio contact with others. Hillary managed to call Louise by radio twice each week.

After much preparation, Hillary and his team of tractor drivers set out on October 14 to chart a route for Fuchs and to arrange for a plane to fly supplies in to depots. The plan was for Hillary to drop a final depot 700 miles inland from Scott Base and then turn back—not to continue on to the South Pole.

A vehicle called a Snow Cat descends Skelton Glacier.

Five men worked closely together on the tractor operation—Jim Bates, Murray Ellis, Peter Mulgrew, Derek Wright, and Hillary. They called themselves the Old Firm. Few people believed tractors could cross the continent, but the greater the doubt others expressed, the greater the determination of the Old Firm. In fact, even though Hillary's men were not supposed to reach the pole, Peter Mulgrew could often be heard mumbling, "Let's go to the pole, Ed."

The Old Firm had trouble late in their expedition. Murray Ellis hurt his back and had to be evacuated. Then Peter Mulgrew fell off the roof of the caboose and broke three ribs. He too had to be rescued. Both men recovered, however, and were later able to resume the expedition.

By the time the team reached its final planned depot—Depot 700—in mid-December, the men felt a sense of satisfaction, realizing they had fulfilled the work required to assist Fuchs in his northward cross from the pole to Scott Base. The morning after Hillary reached Depot 700, he did not leap from his sleeping bag as usual but laid back and took an extra breath, resting in the fact that he had finished his assignment. That good feeling did not last.

Each of Hillary's team members had his own idea for the next stage of the expedition. They were about 500 miles from the South Pole. Hillary wanted to go on. Others thought it was unwise to continue to the pole and risk getting stuck in the ice or running out of fuel. The dissension among team members put Hillary in a foul mood for the rest of the day.

The next morning, spirits were more settled. Hillary received a radio message saying that Fuchs was making progress and would arrive at the pole between Christmas and New Year's Day. Hillary calculated the risks and decided he would go on to the pole, even if he had to do it alone. He believed that Fuchs would not object to the New Zealanders' attempt to continue, as long as they didn't hold up Fuchs's scientific expedition.

Both Fuchs and Hillary later regretted the turn of events that took place. News was leaked that Hillary planned to continue, and the media reacted by declaring the expedition a "Race for the Pole." In his autobiography, Hillary later stated that he never intended to arrive at the pole before Fuchs. He was simply too impatient and too easily bored to stay a month or more at the depot waiting for Fuchs. He wanted to continue to the pole just "for the Hell of it." He wrote:

> I suppose our differences in temperament made for difficulties in communication—I was always impatient for information and quick to make decisions and prepared to change them if something better offered; Bunny [Fuchs] considered his plans with great care and stuck to them with dogged determination once a decision had been made.

Fuchs, too, said that there was no rivalry between the men. There may have been differences in judgment, but Hillary and Fuchs did not view each other as adversaries.

On Christmas Eve, Hillary received a cheerful message from Fuchs. Fuchs and his team had celebrated the holiday with a delicious dinner and brandy while they listened to Radio New Zealand broadcast the voices of their families. Following the festivities, the men started on their way south again.

Meanwhile, Hillary continued to the pole from the other direction. During the final stages of his expedition, he received another message from Fuchs—this time a disheartening one. Fuchs asked Hillary to place another depot between Depot 700 and the pole and to abandon the idea of continuing. Fuchs said that he was low on fuel and wanted to pick up more at the new depot.

Hillary did not like this new plan. He wasn't sure of his own food and fuel supply. The last problem he wanted was to run out of food waiting for Fuchs. Hillary wondered if the media attention had prompted Fuchs's request. He decided to continue to the pole and have a supply plane fly extra fuel into Depot 700 for Fuchs.

The weather worsened. Snow and ice became almost unmanageable. Hillary had the agonizing feeling that he was close to his goal yet unable to reach it. "I have rarely felt a greater sense of helplessness," he wrote in his autobiography.

In desperation, Hillary decided to lighten his load by getting rid of excess food and fuel. Off he went over the last 70 miles to the pole, leaving the reserves in a pile on the white expanse.

On January 4, 1958, Hillary's team reached the South

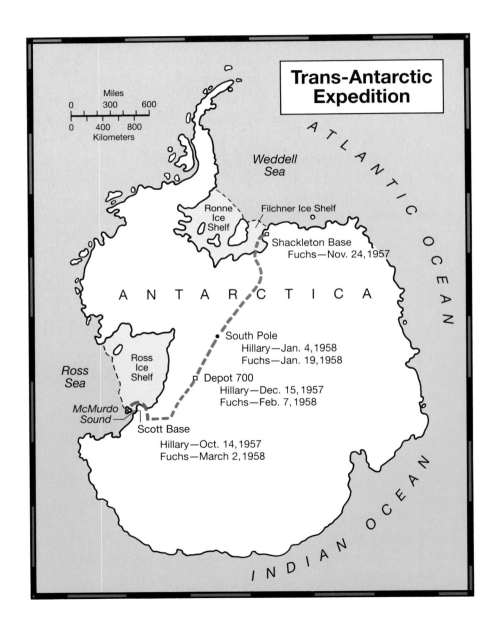

Trans-Antarctic
Expedition

Miles

0   300   600

0   400   800
Kilometers

ATLANTIC OCEAN

Weddell
Sea

Ronne
Ice
Shelf

Filchner Ice Shelf

Shackleton Base
Fuchs—Nov. 24, 1957

ANTARCTICA

South Pole
Hillary—Jan. 4, 1958
Fuchs—Jan. 19, 1958

Depot 700
Hillary—Dec. 15, 1957
Fuchs—Feb. 7, 1958

Ross
Sea

Ross
Ice
Shelf

McMurdo
Sound

Scott Base
Hillary—Oct. 14, 1957
Fuchs—March 2, 1958

INDIAN OCEAN

Pole. Journalists who had flown in to await the teams now bombarded the "winners" of the supposed race. The *Chicago Daily News* reported:

> Sir Edmund Hillary, conqueror of Mount Everest, and his dead tired expedition reached the South Pole today and fell asleep on the spot. They were winners of an Antarctic race and the first men to trek to the Pole in 46 years.

Instead of flying back to McMurdo Sound from the pole, Hillary asked to be flown back to Depot 700 so that he could help navigate Fuchs's last push. Fuchs and his team members arrived at the pole 16 days after Hillary did. They had to move fast to continue all the way to McMurdo Sound before winter was again upon them.

By March 2, Fuchs's 2,180-mile expedition was completed, and Hillary said a last good-bye to Fuchs and his crew. They went on for a hero's welcome in England. Hillary was glad to have represented New Zealand on this international crossing and even more content to be returning to his family in Auckland.

Hillary—briefing reporters in Chicago—shows a picture of the elusive yeti, as well as equipment he will use on the trip to search for the creature.

CHAPTER SEVEN

ON THE YETI TRAIL

AFTER THE ARDUOUS ANTARCTIC EXPEDITION, Hillary returned to his family in Auckland. Instead of chopping away at icebergs and maneuvering around crevasses, he sat at a desk and concentrated on writing a book entitled *No Latitude for Error,* his tale of running tractors to the South Pole. During pauses in his writing, he spent hours reacquainting himself with his children. Upon Hillary's return from Antarctica, Peter, age four, didn't recognize his father. But little by little, the family nested together again. They led a simple life without luxuries and spent vacations sleeping in the wilderness in their favorite accommodation: a tent.

In 1959 Hillary traveled with Louise to the United States, where he was to receive an Explorer of the Year award from *Argosy* magazine. While en route, Hillary was asked to travel to Chicago and work on an educational television program produced by Field Enterprises

Educational Corporation, the publishers of *World Book* encyclopedia. At dinner one evening, Hillary chatted with Field Enterprises' public relations director, John Dienhart, about his dream for future expeditions and a return to Nepal. He confided to Dienhart his dream of searching for the Himalayan *yeti,* the Abominable Snowman, while at the same time undertaking geographical surveys and scientific research on the effects of high altitude on the human body.

Dienhart was enthralled with the idea and thought perhaps Field Enterprises could help fund the expedition. He asked Hillary to send him a full proposal as soon as possible. Hillary returned to New Zealand and promptly forgot about the idea, never expecting his dream to come true. Dienhart, on the other hand, did not forget and made a long-distance phone call to Hillary, reminding him of the proposal. Hillary wrote down his plans, sent them off, and soon received another call asking him to return to Chicago to present the project to the board of directors at Field Enterprises. The result was a $125,000 grant toward a three-phase project. Hillary would orchestrate this expedition with experts on animals and experts on human physiology.

In September 1960, when Hillary was 41 years old, he met with a team in Kathmandu, Nepal. Team members organized 18 tons of supplies and split into two groups: a yeti party, which would head into the Rolwaling Valley, and a scientific party, which would move into the Everest region to carry out physiological research on people.

During the first phase of the expedition, Hillary explored the Rolwaling Valley, following clues about the yeti offered by Sherpas. The team examined suspicious oversized tracks, looked at skins thought to be yeti skins, and even escorted a Sherpa and his alleged yeti scalp and skins from the Khumbu to Chicago, Paris, and London.

Zoologists, anthropologists, and other scientists inspected the scalp and skins. They eventually agreed that the scalp had been molded from the skin of a serow, a Tibetan goat, and that the alleged yeti skins came from a Tibetan blue bear. Hillary's team was unable to find any proof that the yeti existed. While some Sherpas and westerners remained convinced that the yeti lived in hiding high above any human habitat, Hillary's conclusion was that the animal was most likely mythical.

The second phase of the expedition involved high-altitude research directed by Dr. Griffith Pugh, who had accompanied the 1953 Everest expedition. Hillary and Pugh wanted to learn how and why people's bodies adapt to thin air and to determine the maximum altitude at which people can survive. Hillary, Pugh, and their team of doctors, builders, scientists, and Sherpas built an insulated hut at 19,100 feet so that the team could carry on research during winter. Pugh studied physical adaptations to high altitude, including heart rate, oxygen intake, and dehydration.

For the third and final phase, the climbers on the team attempted to climb a peak called Makalu without using extra oxygen. Hillary himself had to abandon the climb after the altitude hurt blood vessels in his brain. He ended up with sharp pains on the side of his head, blurred speech and vision, and lack of balance. Doctors worried that Hillary's condition would worsen if he did not descend, so Hillary regretfully agreed.

Hillary stayed in touch with the other climbers who continued their summit attack. Strong winds slowed the ascent. Finally, all hope of reaching the summit was abandoned when the collapse of one exhausted team member, Peter Mulgrew, turned the expedition into a rescue operation. Mulgrew developed pulmonary edema, or water in the lungs, and doubled over in the snow. Later he blacked out and had to be carried down to camp by Sherpas. He was taken by helicopter to Kathmandu. Mulgrew also suffered such terrible frostbite to his fingers and feet that he had to spend months in the hospital. Doctors were unable to save his feet. Both had to be amputated, and Mulgrew was fitted with two artificial limbs.

Despite the failed summit attempt and the inauthentic yeti remains, this expedition was nonetheless rewarding for Hillary. Through it he found something more meaningful than all of his adventures—something unexpected that would help fulfill him for the rest of his life.

One evening, during his Rolwaling Valley exploration, Hillary sat around a campfire with his Sherpa friends, discussing the Sherpas' life. Despite their hospitable, friendly, hardworking nature, the Sherpas had little material wealth. They lived without heat, electricity, or plumbing, in mud and wood houses. They ate a limited diet of meat, milk, and butter from the yak; pota-toes, barley meal, tea, and homemade beer. The only medicines available to them were herbal cures pre-scribed by Tibetan Buddhist monks. Their outside com-munications came through messengers running from village to village. Sherpa men were all farmers. The only other employ-ment opportunities they had were as porters and guides for moun-taineering expeditions.

> **"PEOPLE IN THE KHUMBU VALLEY HAD NEVER HAD EDUCATION."**

Hillary asked the Sherpas what they needed most. They answered that they needed a lo-cal school. Hillary agreed with the Sherpas. Without edu-cation, Sherpa youths had a limited future in the modern world. Because Hillary cared so much about the Sherpas who had helped him on the mountains, he decided to find a way to give the Sherpas a school. Education would help them become more involved in their own govern-ment, develop their own health-care plans, and improve their agriculture and standard of living.

When Hillary outlined his plan for a new school in Khumjung, the village elders were enthusiastic. So were the children. One boy named Kalden, the only child who could read and write at that time, even drew up a peti-tion, signed by all of the Khumjung children, requesting that Hillary go ahead with the building plan.

In 1961 Hillary's plan became solid, and he persuaded Field Enterprises to finance it. With an aluminum hut do-nated by the Indian Aluminium Company in India, with transport furnished by the International Red Cross, and enthusiastic Sherpa hands, the one-room aluminum school building was erected in six days. One of Hillary's colleagues, Desmond Doig, built seesaws and a swing for

Hillary wondered how he could best help the Sherpa children.

the schoolyard—things never before seen in the Khumbu—
and both parents and children lined up to try them.

On June 11, 1961, the school building was officially
blessed by monks from Tengpoche Monastery. A proces-
sion led by the abbot weaved its way to the school with
trumpets and drums. The monks marched clockwise
around the building twice, while the abbot recited protection prayers for the school. One Sherpa raised the
Nepalese flag, and—borrowing a western tradition—
another placed red ribbon across the main entrance.
Hillary was asked to do the official cutting. He said a few
enthusiastic words and snipped the ribbon. The audience
broke into applause.

To this first school of the Khumbu Valley ran 45 students eager to get inside, settle cross-legged on the wooden
floor, and start writing Nepali letters with chalk on indi-
vidual boards. "People in the Khumbu Valley had never
had education. In fact, they never knew an education system existed in Nepal because their region is just so isolated," said a former Khumjung student named Ang Rita.

Hillary was able to give to the Sherpas a gift that would
most benefit their whole society. But this was just the be-
ginning of Hillary's involvement in Sherpa life.

A Buddhist stupa, or shrine, adorned with prayer flags

CHAPTER EIGHT

KATAS AND BUTTER TEA

DURING THE BUILDING OF THE KHUMJUNG SCHOOL in 1961, Hillary met a Sherpa man, Mingma Tsering, who was energetic and hardworking. The two became fast friends. Hillary hired Mingma to be his sirdar on future expeditions and projects. The two men worked well together; they trusted each other. Hillary always felt at home with Mingma and his wife, Ang Douli, and their three sons.

"To me, the most important [person] of all is my old friend Mingma Tsering," said Hillary in a *National Geographic* interview years after he met Mingma. "Without Mingma's organization and authority among the Sherpas, I could have done nothing."

Every time Hillary went up to the Khumbu, Mingma waited for him along the trail. With katas—white ceremonial scarves—and chang, Mingma offered Hillary a warm welcome. Ang Douli often packed up food and met

Mingma and Hillary on the trail a half day's journey from her home. Or she churned butter, brewed tea with a touch of salt, and boiled potatoes and eggs as a welcoming snack for the man who had changed Sherpa life.

Whenever Hillary entered Mingma and Ang Douli's Khunde village home, he had to bend at the neck and shoulders to climb the steep, dark stairway from the animals' stall on the first floor to the large gathering room on the second. The wooden steps almost swayed under the bulk of the honored guest. Hillary ducked his head under the door frame and appeared in the dim light of Ang Douli's kitchen. Ang Douli made a slight bow, her palms pressed against each other in front of her heart. Smiles stretched across the room. Hillary took his seat of honor—the one against the window, closest to the warmth of the stove—and Ang Douli offered him tea in a clean china cup with a lid.

Temba—Mingma and Ang Douli's deaf son—always rushed to embrace the great family friend. Temba communicated with Hillary through made-up sign language that Hillary had come to understand. Through Hillary's help, Temba had apprenticed under a famous Sherpa artist and had learned to paint traditional landscapes that he sold to trekkers. Temba always loved to pull out his latest painting to show Hillary his progress.

Many villagers also came to Mingma and Ang Douli's home to bring Hillary gifts. They came in streams to thank Hillary and make him comfortable in the Himalayan world that he had joined.

Ang Douli

The Sherpas called Hillary *Burrah Sahib,* which means "great man." "He is a very good man. For Sherpa people, Burrah Sahib is better than King," declared Mingma using his best English. Although Hillary was often away from his own family, he was nevertheless considered to be part of the Sherpa family in the Khumbu.

After the school was built, Hillary returned to New Zealand, content to go on small adventures with Louise and their children: Peter, Sarah, and now the youngest child, Belinda. They hiked and skied in the New Zealand mountains, swam in the Pacific Ocean, and camped in the Australian outback.

Tenzing Norgay visits with the Hillary children—Peter, Belinda, and Sarah—in January 1963.

"Big expeditions are rarely as much fun as small ones—the logistics tend to overshadow the good fellowship and the personal involvement. I have enjoyed all my small expeditions but never more so than when my family has been along," wrote Hillary in his autobiography.

In December 1961, Hillary and his family were invited to spend a year in Chicago. In return for the financial support Hillary had received from Field Enterprises, he had agreed to give a lecture tour in the United States. Louise and the children settled into suburban life outside Chicago. Hillary flew on weeklong trips to other cities, lecturing about his adventures and about Sherpa life. He returned on weekends. Hillary was offered an advisory position by Sears Roebuck and Company. He served as an expert on camping equipment.

In June 1962, the Hillarys piled into a large American station wagon with a camper trailer hooked on behind and drove across the United States and Canada. Hillary had been commissioned by the U.S. secretary of agriculture to do a report on the American national parks and forests. So the family visited many of them, traveling all the way to Alaska. The children aged three, six, and seven, were already experienced campers. At the end of 1962, Hillary finished his lecture tour and returned with his family to New Zealand.

Over the next three years, Hillary spent a great deal of time planning new projects in Nepal. The Sherpas had asked for more schools and also needed a fresh water pipeline, bridges across the Dudh Kosi and the Imja

Khola Rivers, and medical centers. Both Field Enterprises and Sears Roebuck were interested in funding Hillary's projects.

He returned to Nepal in 1963 and 1964 with a team of mountaineers who wanted to climb in the Himalayas and assist in constructing schools, bridges, and medical centers. This system brought help to the Sherpas, while at the same time introducing westerners to the Himalayas. Through Hillary's books and lectures, people in the western world learned about Sherpa life. Many westerners volunteered to help Hillary in the Khumbu or to give money for the projects there.

In December 1966, the entire Hillary family packed backpacks with woolens and sturdy hiking shoes and set off for their first trip together in the Khumbu. Hillary was already in the mountains helping to build a hospital in Khunde. Louise and the children, together with friend Lois Pearl and her three daughters, left New Zealand and flew to Kathmandu. On December 7, the two women and six children took the Royal Nepal Airlines flight from Kathmandu to Lukla, the only mountain airport at the time. Hillary had sponsored the airport-building project; the Sherpas had stomped out the landing field with their own feet. Hillary, Lois Pearl's husband, Max, and a multitude of Sherpa friends awaited the families at Lukla. Mingma and Ang Douli were open-armed and became instant friends with the children.

The weather was frosty that season, and the children were bundled in layers of down. Despite the cold, the

The Lukla airport. Hillary sponsored the airport-building project in the early 1960s.

thin atmosphere, and foreign foods, the children rarely complained. Every morning, Sherpas woke the party with offers of hot tea and hard cookies. That was the signal that the trekkers had to pull themselves from the warmth of their sleeping bags—the hardest part of the day—and get ready for an early morning jaunt.

As December grew darker and colder and the families climbed higher and higher, they faced gusts of sharp wind and nights of early retreat into the tents. They passed the time singing and telling jokes. Edmund had never forgotten the stories that his father had told about Jimmy Job,

Louise, Edmund, and a Sherpa friend, 1970

and he carried on this storytelling tradition with his children. Despite the sharp chill and food that tasted like charcoal, the families couldn't have been happier.

Christmas Eve was spent at Tengpoche Monastery, where the head lama (Buddhist teacher), an old friend of

Hillary's, invited them all to share Sherpa tea, potatoes, and soup. The families huddled around a fire and sang Christmas carols.

On December 28, the party had to say good-bye to their Sherpa friends, exchange white scarves of friendship, and turn back down the trail. Descending through villages, rhododendron trees, and yak pastures, the families hiked in silent sadness. The Hillarys knew they would return, but they would miss the icy peaks and laughing Sherpas.

In 1972 Hillary formally established the Himalayan Trust, his funding organization for the Sherpas. He asked an American expatriate journalist, Elizabeth Hawley, to help administer the trust through an office in Kathmandu.

Problems that troubled the Sherpas troubled other poor people as well. Hillary was gradually becoming more concerned about the social, political, and environmental problems of the entire world. He began to ask big governments to help poorer nations. Hillary's lectures now included discussions about population growth, environmental conservation, human rights, political corruption, and poverty. He was occasionally criticized for talking outside his area of expertise, but he continued to speak out about social injustice.

In January 1975, the entire Hillary family left its New Zealand home and moved to Kathmandu to spend a full year in Nepal. They rented a house, bought a car, and lived in the slow flow of Kathmandu society.

Sarah Hillary, now going on 20, spent some time in Kathmandu and then returned to university in New

Zealand. Peter, a year older, set off with a friend to travel around India. Louise and Belinda took Nepali lessons. Edmund flew up into the mountains to begin building a new hospital in Phaphlu village. Louise and Belinda planned to join him weeks later.

On March 31, 1975, Edmund woke early in Phaphlu with great excitement. Along with Louise's parents and his brother, Rex, he awaited the arrival of his wife and daughter. Louise and Belinda's plane was scheduled to take off early from Kathmandu.

Edmund prepared tents and sleeping bags for Louise and Belinda as he listened for the small Pilatus Porter plane. The plane was late; he wondered what was causing the delay: low cloud cover? weight overload? slow take-off preparations?

At 9:00 A.M., Edmund heard a low roar coming up into the hills, but it was not the sound of the Pilatus Porter. A helicopter readied to land, and Edmund knew that something was wrong. He went to meet the helicopter and out climbed Elizabeth Hawley. Her face was strained. "I'm terribly sorry Ed, but Louise's plane crashed on takeoff."

"Are they alive?" asked Hillary.

"I don't think so," replied Hawley.

Edmund had imagined that if anyone were going to die early, it would be him, not his wife and daughter. Accompanied by Mingma Tsering, Elizabeth Hawley, and Rex, Edmund flew back in the helicopter to Kathmandu and asked the pilot to take him to the crash site.

In his book *Ascent,* Hillary wrote, "We circled near the

Kathmandu airport and slowly descended to the paddy fields where a ring of people were surrounding a burnt and battered wreck. I waded across a small stream and over to the site of the crash—to the last resting place of the two people I had loved most."

He wrote: "For me the most rewarding moments have not always been the great moments. For what can surpass a tear on departure, joy on your return, and a trusting hand in yours?" He had such a loving closeness with Louise, such deep affection for his daughter Belinda. Now their handclasps were gone forever.

Pilgrims wash themselves at Varanasi, the holiest city in India.

CHAPTER NINE

PILGRIMAGE BY SPEEDBOAT

FOR PEOPLE WHO LIVE IN INDIA AND PRACTICE THE Hindu religion, traveling the length of the Ganges River is a sacred pilgrimage. The voyage from the mouth of the river that opens at the Bay of Bengal to the source of the river at Badrinath, in the Himalayan mountains, is thought to bring the human and the divine together. Although they were not Hindus, Hillary and Louise had planned for years to make this trip together. Now, Hillary knew he had to find the strength within himself to continue living—and he decided to make the trip without her.

Hillary began his "Ocean to Sky" trip up the Ganges River as a speedboat expedition. Hindu worshippers normally walk the banks of the river. Many Hindus thought that by motoring upriver, Hillary was challenging the gods. They doubted he could reach the river's source.

Hillary was more optimistic. On August 24, 1977, when he was 58 years old, he set out up the Ganges. With the support of the Indian government he formed a team of expert speedboat drivers, experienced mountain climbers (including his son, Peter), local river guides, and an expert on Indian religions and languages. As always, Hillary's friend and sirdar, Mingma Tsering, also went along.

Operating three speedboats, the *Ganga,* the *Kiwi,* and the *Air India,* the team hoped to travel upriver against the rapids as far as possible. Then they would continue their journey on foot to Badrinath.

As the speedboat team set out, they met up with the local *pujare,* or holy man, and asked him for a blessing. Wrapped in sheer cloth, his wispy white beard and long hair caught in the wind rising off the river, the holy man approached the boats with his ceremonial instruments. He marked Hillary's head with a streak of crimson powder and chanted prayers as he broke coconuts on the bow of each boat. Hillary felt a warm sense of comfort from this ceremony.

August was monsoon season in India, a time of fierce rainstorms. The Ganges was ferocious. After only a few hours of river travel, the men were initiated into the realm of the sacred waters. In other words, they got soaked to the bone.

The speedboats passed old wooden sailboats with tattered maroon sails. Wildlife moved around them—egrets flying across the sky and camouflaged tigers pacing the banks of the river."You are very lucky, Sir," said a local forest guide who accompanied Hillary through dangerous tiger country. "Rarely does anyone see one tiger let alone two. It is indeed a very good omen for your journey up Mother Ganga."

The team stopped for two days in Calcutta, India, approximately 60 miles from the start. When they were ready to pull out of the port, they looked up to see a crowd of curious onlookers on a bridge. One Indian team member estimated that at least two million people stood watching and waving. All India Radio had spread the news of the river expedition, and villagers all along the river were captivated by the idea of this modern pilgrimage.

Pilgrims at the Ganges

There was much handshaking and smiling as Hillary greeted admirers. A young boy was brought forward, and Hillary signed the child's autograph book. This kind gesture nearly caused a riot. As soon as the crowd saw Hillary give his autograph, everyone wanted one. One policeman, acting with inappropriate force, rammed his rifle butt against the chest of a young man in front of the crowd. The injured man became irate and began to stir up trouble. One official wisely asked Hillary if he would be willing to shake hands with the angry man. Hillary moved toward the man, tapped him on the shoulder, and held out his hand. The man whipped around—peered into Hillary's face—then broke into laughter and shook hands. With that, Hillary wasted no time getting back on his boat and out to the middle of the river.

The Ganges River is six miles wide in places. The speedboat drivers, Jon and Mike Hamilton and Jim Wilson, had to cope with fast rapids one minute, shallow sandbanks the next. When a boat hit a sandbank, team members were often sent hurtling forward. Some even flipped out of the boat.

Pushing forward against the river by day and camping by night, the team had few worries. One hardship, however, was the constant crowd of admirers. Even when the team tried to find an isolated campsite, locals found them. Shy villagers hid behind trees; brave ones marched right into camp and stared at the team members.

Hillary was as gracious as possible. Peter, however, was not happy being in the shadow of his famous father.

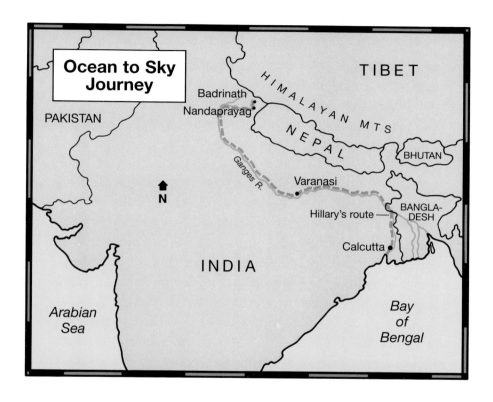

He had taken his own Himalayan adventures and risks and wanted to be known for those.

On September 8, the team reached Varanasi, the halfway point in their journey. Varanasi, where Hindus come to wash themselves of their impurities, is the holiest city in India. Hillary and his friends worried that the Indians might be insulted at the sight of speedboats traveling in sacred waters. To their surprise, the city put on a special blessing ceremony for the continued success of the journey.

Another pujare appeared—a young man with wild tangled hair, bright eyes, and muscular shoulders. He stared into the sky and chanted with great energy, tossing flower petals and ringing a bell as he asked the river gods to protect the expedition team. The ceremony quieted Hillary and caused him to put aside his personal sadness for a while.

After 1,500 miles and more than a month of river travel, the team met their greatest obstacle just short of Nandaprayag: a 10-foot waterfall. The rest of the expedition would have to be made on foot. From this point on, the travelers shared the pilgrims' road. The road traversed upward to the Golden Staircase—1,064 stone steps leading to the sacred lake of Hemkund at 15,000 feet. Here, the weather was cold. Pilgrims wrapped themselves in cotton cloth and blankets—scant protection from the sharp wind. Some of the more adventurous team members leaped into the frigid lake.

They descended and continued on to the sacred town of Badrinath, then set off up a glacier to the snow-covered summit, Akash Parbat. On October 10, the team set up base camp at 15,000 feet. Anticipating the challenge of a climb, Hillary moved slowly, trying to adjust to the altitude. But he did not realize the extent of his fatigue. After a treacherous climb to the high camp, Hillary collapsed at 18,000 feet and crawled into his tent. Too tired to eat, he spent the night having nightmares.

Peter Hillary and a few other climbers felt impatient. They went on ahead while another group stayed at camp for a day of rest. Edmund Hillary, too tired to move and plagued with head and body aches, stayed in his tent. Dr. Mike Gill examined Edmund but couldn't determine any serious illness. He injected Hillary with a painkiller that made him pass out.

Hillary doesn't remember what happened next. Team members tried to wake him the next morning and found him unconscious, suffering from altitude sickness. Leaving Hillary in his sleeping bag inside his tent, team members picked up the tent and carried him down the steep trail. A rescue helicopter waiting in Badrinath rushed him to a hospital. There, Hillary began his recovery from severe swelling of the brain. His fate could have been worse; altitude sickness can kill victims who do not descend quickly enough. Hillary did suffer from memory loss, and from then on, he could never again climb above 14,000 feet.

Hillary visits a school-building site at Tengpoche.

CHAPTER TEN

A VOICE FOR OUR PLANET

FROM TUAKAU TO EVEREST TO THE SOUTH POLE, up the Ganges and into the Khumbu Valley, Edmund Hillary's life has been one of constant motion. Many people look upon Hillary as a hero, but this is a title the man himself denies.

"I'm not a hero at all. I firmly believe that I am the creation of the media and the public. I am a person of very modest abilities....This heroic figure that exists in the public mind doesn't exist at all," Hillary told an interviewer.

Hillary has always thought of himself as an ordinary man whose only special qualities were persistence and energy. In search of satisfaction and accomplishment, Hillary has driven himself to overcome the difficulties of any task ahead of him.

But this drive, coupled with his strong ethic to help his fellow human beings and preserve natural wilderness, has won Hillary the reputation of a hero whether he

105

wants it or not. Hillary has been hailed by royalty, celebrated by prime ministers, praised by fellow explorers, and cheered by admirers.

Elizabeth Hawley, who has worked with Hillary since the early 1970s, claims: "I think he's one of the finest people I've ever known because he has a very high ethical standard and he is very concerned to help his friends."

The Sherpas, of course, do not think of Hillary as an ordinary man. Some of them even believe that he is the reincarnation of a Buddhist deity.

Sherpa villagers drink butter tea.

Edmund Hillary and Tenzing Norgay in 1983, 30 years after their famous climb

Ordinary man or hero, Hillary's contributions to the world have exceeded most people's. During the 1980s he returned to Nepal year after year—to ensure that his projects were running smoothly and to help transfer responsibility for the projects to educated and motivated young Sherpas who had finished college and gone back to their villages. Because of the programs Hillary had put in place, the returning natives were able to find work in their own communities as park rangers, teachers, doctors, and trek leaders. Hillary continued to lecture around the world and to raise funds for the Himalayan Trust. He hired a Sherpa, Ang Rita, to help Elizabeth Hawley in the trust's Kathmandu office.

Because Hillary's dedication to the people of the Himalayan region had always been so fervent, in the 1980s New Zealand's prime minister made Hillary high commissioner to India. As a diplomat, Hillary was able to become even more involved in finding solutions to the social, political, and environmental problems that concerned him.

Environmental destruction of the Everest region has plagued Hillary. He has often felt responsible for an influx of tourism to the Everest area, which resulted from the building of the Lukla airport. Every year, from March until November, thousands of trekkers and climbers fly into the region and take over the trails. They sometimes abandon used equipment and trash on the mountainside without considering the impact on the environment. Development and logging in the region have led to erosion.

"When we climbed Everest," commented Hillary in an interview, "we just heaved all our rubbish outside our camp on the way up the mountain. We never even thought about it because, in those days, conservation simply hadn't become a proper cause. I hope that I wouldn't do the same thing again....I really do look back on it with quite a lot of shame.

"What depresses me is that the modern mountaineer who is meant to be in the forefront of conservation seems just as careless as we were all those years ago. I would like to, and have recommended to the Nepalese Government that Everest be closed down for a period of five years to let the mountain regenerate. Nature has a great ability to regenerate."

This idea has not been met with applause from everyone—especially ambitious climbers who have not yet had a chance to climb the tallest mountain in the world. Hillary understands their ambition but also wants to preserve the land. "All of us who love the mountains, rivers, and

Stunted plant growth on a Himalayan hillside

This tree nursery is part of an effort to fight erosion in the Himalayas.

deserts have a strong responsibility to ensure that development is carefully guided and that nature is not simply enjoyed, but carefully preserved," said Hillary.

He has became involved in creating Sagarmatha National Park in the Everest area as a means of protecting the land. He has helped open nurseries to grow new trees and prevent erosion on slopes that have been harvested

Edmund rests with longtime friend Mingma Tsering and son Peter during a mountain trek.

Hillary and some Sherpa children

for lumber. Hillary has had help from active friends and colleagues, including Canadian Zeke O'Connor and American Larry Witherbee. These men visit the Khumbu regularly with Hillary to consult on projects, secure foreign assistance, discuss land maintenance with Sherpa leaders, and prevent illegal cutting of trees.

The Sherpas are unsure of their future. They depend on tourism for employment: guiding trekkers and climbers is the most profitable way for Sherpas to make a living. There has always been a trade-off. With foreigners come trash and erosion, but so too come better jobs, better education, electricity, and medical care. The question Sherpas now face is how to decrease the destruction of their region without sacrificing the benefits—and how to assert cultural and environmental preservation above the personal interests of trekkers and climbers.

Until Hillary introduced an educational system into the area, conservation was not even a topic of interest in Nepal. Today, Sherpas work together to find solutions to their environmental and economic problems. Alternative fuel sources are being explored, and Sherpas are organizing their own fund-raising campaigns. To save energy, some Sherpas use solar panels donated by westerners; others make a habit of going to bed early, to save electricity. Schoolchildren have been taught to plant young trees and to avoid throwing garbage into their forests. This environmental consciousness was introduced by Hillary and is now maintained by concerned Sherpa leaders.

Hillary helped create the Sagarmatha National Park to protect the Himalayan wilderness. Sagarmatha is the Nepalese name for Mount Everest.

Hillary's adventures began in the realm of his imagination. When he was a child—too young to change the real world—he was a hero in his fantasies. Then, when he was old enough, he followed his inspiration and pushed himself to explore uncharted lands. He discovered that life in the outdoors offered him the exhilaration he sought.

Hillary never led an ordinary life with a steady nine-to-five job. He never earned a living from just one source but from a combination of sources: beekeeping, testing outdoor equipment, lecturing throughout the world, and writing adventure books. For Edmund Hillary, there was always another challenge ahead—and his greatest challenge was to help the Sherpa people of Nepal.

Hillary learned to live with the loss of his wife and daughter. He watched his other daughter, Sarah, and his son, Peter, leave home and start families of their own.

In December 1990, Hillary remarried. His new wife, an energetic and friendly woman named June Mulgrew, was formerly married to Hillary's good friend and travel companion Peter Mulgrew. Hillary and Louise maintained a friendship with the Mulgrew couple until the early deaths of both Louise and Peter. June has always been welcomed in the Khumbu Valley and has become a strong partner in Hillary's projects. In her own right, June was an energetic trek leader, taking women's adventure groups to Nepal. She set a quick pace up the steepest trails and kept the groups cheerful with her humor. Hillary and June had a small family wedding in their Auckland home.

In the spring of 1990, Hillary took another trek to the Khumbu, not unlike his treks of former years. He asked his trusted companions from New Zealand to come and help rebuild monastery roofs and renovate schools. Hillary, together with Zeke O'Connor and Larry Witherbee, inspected many schools, medical centers, and tree nurseries.

Sherpas often come to Hillary with requests for more schools, more medical centers, and college scholarships for bright Sherpa students. Hillary considers every

Edmund and his wife, June Mulgrew, 1991

request, discusses it with his colleagues, and then grants or denies the request, depending on its urgency.

Year after year, Hillary's trips have been similar. But 1990 was the last year Hillary would take a long trek from village to village. Hillary was 71 years old, and mountain hiking had become difficult. On his next visit he decided that he would helicopter up into the Khumbu.

Edmund Hillary does not often look back on his life. He has so much ahead of him—project after project still waiting to be accomplished. Someday, the world will say good-bye to Edmund Hillary, but the echo of his life, his generosity, and his spirit will be heard forever.

SOURCES

10 Sir Edmund Hillary, *High Adventure* (New York: E. P. Dutton & Co., 1955), 232.

13 Sir Edmund Hillary, *Nothing Venture, Nothing Win* (New York: Coward, McCann & Geoghegan, Inc., 1975), 308.

16 June Carlile, interview with author, January 1991.

16 Carlile interview.

16 Carlile interview.

17 Sir Edmund Hillary, interview with author, November 1989.

18 Carlile interview.

19 Hillary, *Nothing Venture, Nothing Win*, 20.

20 Ibid., 27.

21 Hillary interview.

23 Carlile interview.

25 Hillary, *Nothing Venture, Nothing Win*, 25.

30 George Lowe, interview with author, January 1991.

37 Ralph Izzard, *An Innocent on Everest* (New York: E. P. Dutton & Co., Inc., 1954), 217.

38–39 Television New Zealand, "This Is Your Life," 1986.

41 Tom Stobart, *I Take Pictures for Adventure* (Garden City, N.Y.: Doubleday & Co., 1958), 221.

45 Ibid., 246.

45 James Morris, "To the Summit," *London Times*, July 1953, 22.

45 Hillary, *Nothing Venture, Nothing Win*, 149.

46 Tenzing Norgay, *Tiger of the Snows* (New York: G. P. Putnam's Sons, 1955), 222.

47 Morris, "To the Summit," 22.

47 Sir John Hunt with Edmund Hillary, *The Conquest of Everest* (New York: E. P. Dutton & Co., 1954), 229.

49 Ibid., 199.

50 Hillary interview.

50 Hunt and Hillary, *Conquest of Everest*, 204.

57 Hillary, *Nothing Venture, Nothing Win*, 167.

57 Ibid., 168.

64 Sir Vivian Fuchs, interview with author, January 1991.

66 Sir Vivian Fuchs, *A Time to Speak: An Autobiography*, (Oswestry, Shropshire, England: Anthony Nelson, 1990), 233.

71 Hillary, *Nothing Venture, Nothing Win*, 211.

72 Fuchs, *A Time to Speak*, 243.

72 Hillary, *Nothing Venture, Nothing Win*, 209.

73 Ibid., 229.

75 Ibid, 215.

83 Ang Rita, interview with author, April 1990.

85 National Geographic, "Return to Everest," video, 1985.

88 Mingma Tsering, interview with author, April 1990.

89 Hillary, *Nothing Venture, Nothing Win*, 282.

94 Sir Edmund Hillary and Peter Hillary, *Ascent: Two Lives Explored* (Garden City, N.Y.: Doubleday & Co., 1986), 42.

95 Ibid., 43.

95 Hillary, *Nothing Venture, Nothing Win*, 308.

99 Hillary and Hillary *Ascent*, 59.

105 Hillary interview.

106 Elizabeth Hawley, interview with author, April 1990.

109 Sir Edmund Hillary, "A Practical Suggestion," *Summit: The Mountain Journal,* summer 1991, 10.

111 Ibid.

S E L E C T E D   B I B L I O G R A P H Y

Evans, Charles. *Eye on Everest: A Sketch Book from the Great Everest Expedition.* London: Dennis Dobson, 1955.

Fuchs, Sir Vivian. *A Time to Speak: An Autobiography.* Oswestry, Shropshire, England: Anthony Nelson, 1990.

Fuchs, Sir Vivian, and Sir Edmund Hillary. *The Crossing of Antarctica.* Boston: Little Brown & Co., 1958.

Hillary, Louise. *High Time.* New York: E. P. Dutton & Co., 1974.

Hillary, Louise. *Keep Calm If You Can.* New York: Doubleday & Co., 1964.

Hillary, Sir Edmund. *High Adventure.* New York: E. P. Dutton & Co., 1955.

Hillary, Sir Edmund. *No Latitude for Error.* London: Hodder & Stoughton, 1961.

Hillary, Sir Edmund. *Nothing Venture, Nothing Win.* New York: Coward, McCann & Geoghegan, Inc., 1975.

Hillary, Sir Edmund. *Schoolhouse in the Clouds.* Garden City, N.Y.: Doubleday & Co., 1964.

Hillary, Sir Edmund, and Desmond Doig. *High in the Thin Cold Air.* Garden City, N.Y.: Doubleday & Co., 1962.

Hillary Sir Edmund and Peter Hillary. *Ascent: Two Lives Explored.* Garden City, N.Y.: Doubleday & Co., 1986.

Hillary, Sir Edmund and Peter Hillary. *Two Generations.* London: Hodder and Stoughton, 1984.

Hunt, Sir John, with Sir Edmund Hillary. *The Conquest of Everest.* New York: E. P. Dutton & Co., Inc., 1954.

Izzard, Ralph. *An Innocent on Everest.* New York: E. P. Dutton & Co., Inc., 1954.

Jefferies, Margaret. *Mount Everest National Park. Sagarmatha. Mother of the Universe.* Seattle: The Mountaineers, 1986.

Norgay, Tenzing, with James Ramsey Ullman. *Tiger of the Snows.* New York: G. P. Putnam's Sons, 1955.

Stobart, Tom. *I Take Pictures for Adventure.* Garden City, N.Y.: Doubleday & Co., 1958.

PHOTO ACKNOWLEDGMENTS

The photographs in this book are copyright © Anne B. Keiser, except for the following, which are used by permission of: Archive Photos, p. 2; George Lowe, pp. 6, 58, 62; UPI/Bettmann, pp. 8, 44, 55; UPI/Bettmann Newsphotos, pp. 11, 63, 76; June Carlile/Sir Edmund Hillary, p. 12; June Carlile, pp. 18, 23, 24, 28, 32, 88; Royal Geographical Society, pp. 36, 46, 51, 67, 70; The Bettmann Archive, p. 52; Archive Photos/Express Newspapers, p. 60; Archive Photos/AFP, p. 92; Air-India Library, p.96; and Ruthi Soudack, p. 99. Maps on pages 15, 34–35, 74, and 101 are by Laura Westlund. Front cover photograph of Sir Edmund Hillary is reproduced by permission of UPI/Bettmann. Background photograph on front cover is reproduced by permission of Anne B. Keiser.

Sherpa children in ceremonial dress

A B O U T   T H E   A U T H O R

Whitney Stewart writes fiction and nonfiction, with a special interest in life in the Himalayan Mountains. She has traveled to Tibet, Nepal, and Dharamsala, India, where she lived with a Tibetan family. She has also written a biography of the 14th Dalai Lama of Tibet.

A B O U T   T H E   P H O T O G R A P H E R

Anne B. Keiser grew up in Washington, D.C., and graduated from Middlebury College in Vermont. She was a picture editor and photographer for the National Geographic Society, where she first met and worked with Sir Edmund Hillary. Since then she has returned several times to Nepal to document Hillary's work and the projects supported by his Himalayan Trust.

Whitney Stewart, Edmund Hillary, June Mulgrew, and Anne Keiser

Lerner's **Newsmakers** series:

Muhammad Ali: Champion
Ray Charles: Soul Man
The 14th Dalai Lama: Spiritual Leader of Tibet
Sir Edmund Hillary: To Everest and Beyond